RULE HAIKU

RULE HAIKU
FEDERAL RULES *of* APPELLATE PROCEDURE

॰

Levi Jones

Copyright © Levi Jones, 2018
All Rights Reserved

ISBN 978-0-9998373-2-0 (Hardcover Edition)
ISBN 978-0-9998373-3-7 (EPUB Edition)

Without limiting the rights under copyright reserved above, no part of this publication may be reproduced, stored in or introduced into a retrieval system, or transmitted, in any form or by any means (electronic, mechanical, photocopying, recording, or otherwise), without the prior written permission of the copyright owner.

The scanning, uploading, and distribution of this book via the Internet or via any other means without the permission of the copyright owner is illegal and punishable by law. Please purchase only authorized editions and do not participate in or encourage electronic piracy of copyrightable materials. Your support of the author's rights is appreciated.

For Bonnie

Preface

Donald Leif Rokke decided to do the Reagan administration a favor. In 1986, he compiled a document he titled, "Macro Economics Study, Collection of Data" consisting of five pages of analysis and about twenty pages of magazine and newspaper clippings, and mailed it to the president and other officials. On his tax return that year, Mr. Rokke valued his contribution of research to the government at $250,000 and deducted half of his adjusted gross income, substantially lowering his tax bill. The IRS disagreed with Mr. Rokke's tax calculations, issuing him a deficiency notice and a penalty.

Mr. Rokke's dispute with the IRS made its way through the tax court and up to the U.S. Court of Appeals for the Ninth Circuit. In his appeal, Mr. Rokke argued that, not only were his tax calculations correct, but that he was entitled to be paid his appeal costs because, "the appeals process is so complicated and such a vexatious as well as resource consuming, high stress, traumatic experience." The Ninth Circuit took the IRS's side, ruled against Mr. Rokke, and declined to award him costs. *Rokke v. Commissioner of Internal Revenue*, 2 F.3d 1157 (1993).

Although Mr. Rokke did not win on appeal, he is not alone in finding the appeals process vexatious. This is so despite the best intentions and efforts of many great legal minds that have tried (and are still trying) to create an appeals process that is straightforward and fair. When the Federal Rules of Appellate Procedure were adopted, legal experts such as Professor Harvey L. Zuckman of Saint Louis University hailed them as "a reasonably successful effort on the part of the drafters to choose the best procedures developed by the individual circuits over the years." *An Examination of the Federal Rules of Appellate Procedure*, 13 St. Louis U. L.J. 564 (1969). It may be that even the best set of procedures designed to cover something as multifarious as the federal appeals process is bound to be somewhat vexatious, especially to a newcomer.

The poems in this book, which convert each federal rule of appellate procedure into a haiku, are an attempt to pull some simplicity out of those rules by making them fit within the rules of haiku. You can only squeeze one of these rules into the haiku structure by cutting out most of the nuance, and indeed the simplicity that results is, ultimately, an oversimplification. Nevertheless, I hope that by comparing the haiku with the rule's full text, students, practitioners, and those exceptionally curious about appellate procedure can understand a little more clearly what the drafters intended with each rule, and find themselves a little less vexed. And if the poems don't help, perhaps the images that accompany the poems, which were created by much more talented hands, will do a better job.

Levi Jones

RULE HAIKU

Federal Rules
of
Appellate Procedure

Title I.
Applicability *of* Rules

1.

All courts of appeals
In matters of procedure
Use this set of rules

2.

Courts may suspend rules
To expedite decisions
Or for other cause

TITLE II.
Appeal *from a* Judgment *or* Order *of a* District Court

3.

Notice of appeal

Timely, names parties and court

States what is appealed

4.

Entry of judgment

Clock starts for filing notice

Most get thirty days

5.

Courts may sometimes hear

Discretionary appeals

Ask for permission

6.

Bankruptcy appeals

Like other civil appeals

With just a few quirks

7.

Bond for appeal costs

Or other security

From the appellant

8.

Stay pending appeal

Move in the district court first

Or show why you can't

9.

Criminal release

Appeal pre- or post-sentence

Briefs need not be filed

10.

Record on appeal

Papers filed, transcript, docket

Or agreed statement

11.

Forward the record
When it's complete, with a list
Of the documents

12.

Docket the appeal
File record and tell parties
First jobs of the clerk

12.1

If the district court
Is asked to reconsider
Circuit may remand

Title III.
Appeals *from the* United States Tax Court

13.

Appeal from tax court

File notice with the tax court

Ninety days to file

14.

A tax-court appeal

Ninety days to file notice

Mailing is filing

Title IV.
Review *or* Enforcement *of an* Order *of an* Administrative Agency, Board, Commission, *or* Officer

15.

Agency has ruled
File petition for review
Or for enforcement

15.1.

A party adverse
To NLRB's ruling
Always proceeds first

16.

Record on Review

Agency proceeding docs

They are the same thing

17.

Agency record

In full or selected parts

Forty days to file

18.

Stay pending appeal

Move before agency first

Unless that's pointless

19.

Agency half-wins

Agency drafts court order

Ten days to challenge

20.

All these rules apply

To agency order suits

With some exceptions

Title V.
Extraordinary Writs

21.

Writ of mandamus

Proceeding gets preference

Court may ask for briefs

TITLE VI.
Habeas Corpus; Proceedings In Forma Pauperis

22.

Habeas corpus

Seek writ from district court first

Get certificate

23.

Habeas pending

Prisoner may be locked up,

Transferred, or released

Title VII.
General Provisions

25.

File papers with clerk

Clerk may not refuse on form

Serve and prove you served

26.

Exclude the first day

Count each day, holidays too

Include the last day

26.1.

Disclosure statement

Corporate parties must file

ID all parents

27.

Motion for relief

Single judge may act on it

Respond in ten days

28.

Appellant files brief

Appellee files its own brief

Appellant replies

28.1.

Cross-appeals: four briefs

Principal and response briefs

Two for each party

29.

All friends of the court
May file briefs with leave of court
State whose side you're on

30.

Record's greatest hits

Pulled into the appendix

Just one for the case

31.

Briefs served back and forth

Forty days, then thirty days

Then fourteen days more

32.

Appellees are red

Appellants are blue, other

Filings, different hues

32.1.

Citing opinions

Whether they're published or not

From '07 on

33.

Appeal conference

Try to simplify issues

Discuss settlement

34.

Oral argument

Appellant speaks first and last

Court may close its ears

35.

Unusual case

Inconsistent decisions

Seek en banc hearing

36.

Entry of judgment

When noted on the docket

Parties get copies

37.

Judgment interest

Affirm: from date of judgment

Reverse: it depends

38.

Frivolous appeal

Notice and chance to respond

Just damages, costs

39.

The loser pays costs

Winner files itemized bill

Loser may object

40.

Panel rehearing

Say what facts or law were missed

Fourteen days to seek

41.

Judgment, opinion
A mandate that may be stayed
Pending petitions

42.

Appellant gives up

Dismiss with stipulation

Or motion; pay costs

43.

Substitute parties

When dead or out of office

Or for other cause

44.

Challenging a law?
Tell attorney general
Federal or state

45.

Busy circuit clerk

Runs docket and calendar

Among other things

46.

Court bar admission
Good standing elsewhere,
    vouched for
Misconduct? You're out

47.

Each court's local rules
Consistent with all these rules
And federal law

48.

Special master runs

Ancillary proceedings

By court appointment

List of Images

1. John Singer Sargent, Bather, Florida, 1917
2. Shikibu Terutada, Birds and Flowers of Summer and Autumn, ca. 1550
3. Winslow Homer, A Basket of Clams, 1873
4. "Lion", Folio from the Mantiq al-wahsh (Speech of the Wild Animal) of Ka'b al-Ahbar, 11th-12th century
5. Anonymous, Botanical Study, ca. 1820
6. "Rosette Bearing the Names and Titles of Shah Jahan", Folio from the Shah Jahan Album, ca. 1645
7. Henry Farrar, Winter Scene in Moonlight, 1869
8. Bihzad (attr.), "Dancing Dervishes", Folio from a Divan of Hafiz, ca. 1480
9. Embroidered Mantle Fragment, 3rd-2nd century B.C.
10. Tiffany & Co., Study of a Magnolia Blossom, ca. 1891
11. Charles Demuth, Yellow and Blue, 1915
12. Sir Edward John Poynter, The West Wind, 1866
13. Herbert E. Crowley, A Monument in a Mountainous Landscape 1911–24

2

www.ingramcontent.com/pod-product-compliance
Lightning Source LLC
Chambersburg PA
CBHW041108160426
42811CB00091B/1080